COMICS BUYER'S GUIDE PRESENTS: THE TEAM!

SENIOR EDITOR
Maggie Thompson

EDITOR
Brent Frankenhoff - ext. 13480
brent.frankenhoff@fwmedia.com

DESIGNER
Shawn Williams

ADVERTISING SALES
(800) 726-9966
Shannon Piotrowski - ext. 13380
shannon.piotrowski@fwmedia.com

Amanda Wild - ext. 13653
amanda.wild@fwmedia.com

AD SALES ASSISTANT
Lori Hauser - ext. 13239

PUBLISHER
David Blansfield

EDITORIAL DIRECTOR
Paul Kennedy

F+W MEDIA, INC.
David Nussbaum, Chairman & CEO
James Ogle, CFO
David Blansfield, President
Senior Vice President, Advertising & Sales
David Shiba Senior VP, Manufacturing &
Production, Phil Graham
Executive VP, eMedia, Chad Phelps

Newsstand Circulation
Scott Hill, scott.hill@procirc.com

**TO SUBSCRIBE TO CBG,
CONTACT SUBSCRIBER SERVICES**
386-246-3432
P.O. Box 420235
Palm Coast, FL 32142

EDITORIAL AND AD OFFICE
700 E. State St.
Iola, WI 54990-0001
(715) 445-2214
FAX (715) 445-4087
http://cbgxtra.com
cbg@krause.com

Image source: *Dell Four Color* #386 (Mar 52).
© 1952 The Walt Disney Company. Artist: Carl Barks

Welcome to *Comics Buyer's Guide Presents: 100 Baddest Motherf*#!ers!* Scrooge McDuck, who didn't make our list in part because he's a talking duck, spelled out some of the criteria we used to identify the characters who *did* make the cut. They had to be, as Scrooge said, "tougher than the toughies, and smarter than the smarties!" While we ended up including a few whose I.Q. isn't that high, it's their cunning and never-say-die attitudes that put them in the group. We also included a few guys who may not seem so tough — but they kick butt in *other* ways, as you'll see.

If you picked up the first book in this series, *Comics Buyer's Guide Presents: 100 Sexiest Women of Comics*, you won't have to ask how we came to produce this foray into the world of formidable foes. But, whether or not you have that book (and there may still be copies where you picked up this book), you should know that *Comics Buyer's Guide* is the longest-running magazine about comics in the Western Hemisphere. Begun in 1971 by a teen in East Moline, Ill., *CBG* has brought comics fans and pros news, reviews, auction updates, and commentary for four decades. Subscription and other information appears at left. You can also check out selected back issues free on your iTunes-ready mobile device through the Comics+ app.

These are our choices. Are they yours? Did we leave out (or downgrade) your favorite? Make your case at *CBGXtra.com*, via email to *ohso@krause.com*, or by mail to our editorial offices. Ready ... Aim ...

— *Brent Frankenhoff*

Published by
Krause Publications, a division of F+W Media, Inc.
700 East State Street • Iola, WI 54990-0001
715-445-2214 • 888-457-2873
www.krausebooks.com
To order books or other products call toll-free 1-800-258-0929
or visit us online at www.krausebooks.com or www.Shop.Collect.com

Cover image source: *Power Man and Iron Fist* #50 (Apr 78).
© 1978 Marvel Comics Group, a division of Cadence
Industries Corporation. Artist: Dave Cockrum

ISBN-13: 978-1-4402-3050-9
ISBN-10: 1-4402-3050-1

Cover Design by Shawn Williams
Designed by Shawn Williams
Edited and written by Brent Frankenhoff and Maggie Thompson
Printed in China

krause publications
A division of F+W Media, Inc.

fw media

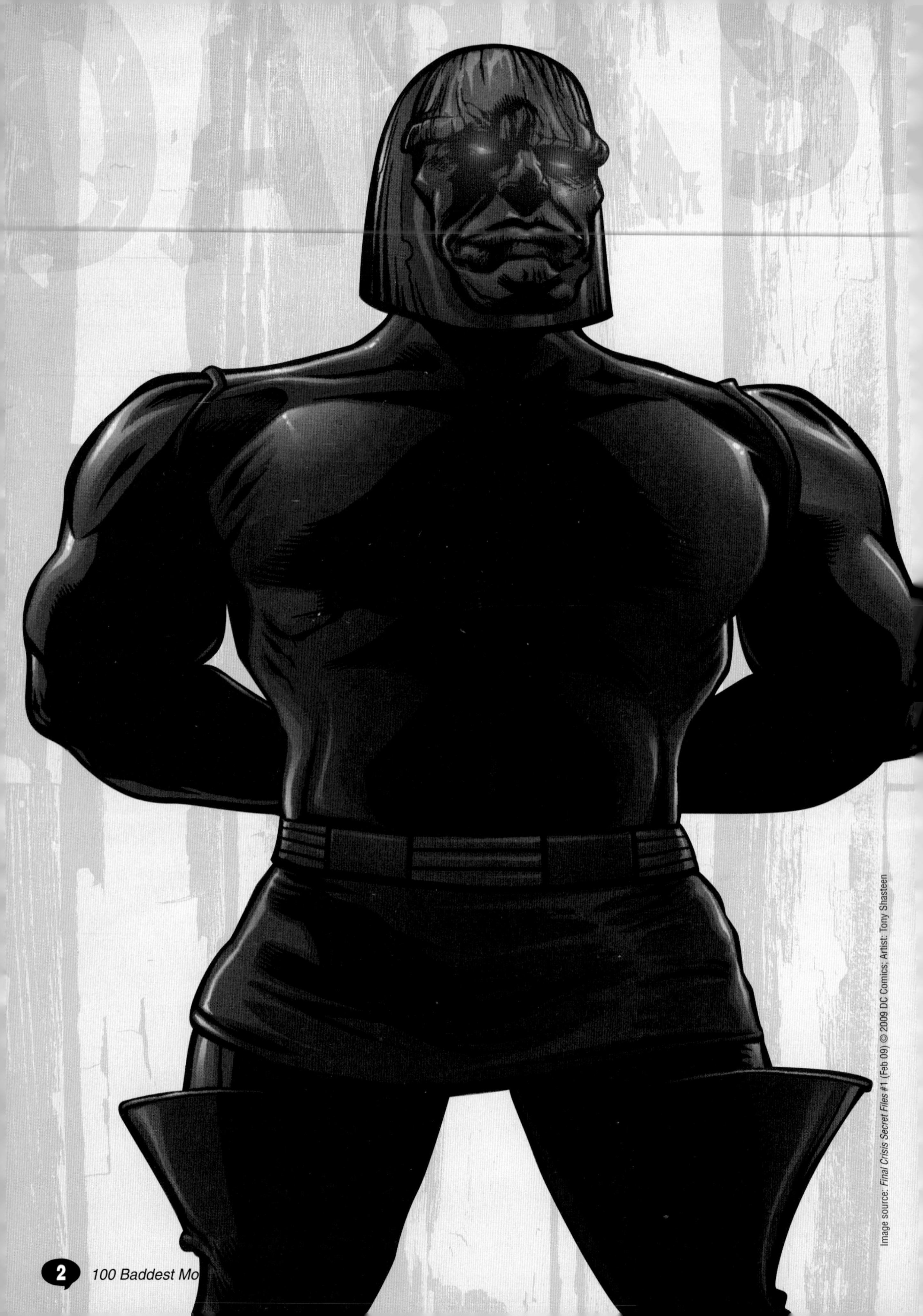

Image source: *Final Crisis Secret Files* #1 (Feb 09) © 2009 DC Comics; Artist: Tony Shasteen

1 DARKSEID

The dark lord of Apokolips is the most menacing figure in the DC Universe — from his stony countenance to his Omega Beam-firing eyes to his vicious machinations in a quest for the Anti-Life Equation. His epic battles have included going toe-to-toe with Superman, but, in his ultimate battle, he faced the unfettered might of his own son: Orion.

WELCOME, MY FRIENDS, TO APOKOLIPS.

I AM ITS MASTER-- DARKSEID THE DESTROYER!

Image source: *Crisis on Infinite Earths* #12 (Mar 86) © 1985 DC Comics, Inc.; Artist: George Pérez

Image source: *The Hunger Dogs* (DC Graphic Novel #4, Mar 86) © 1984 DC Comics, Inc.; Artists: Jack Kirby and various

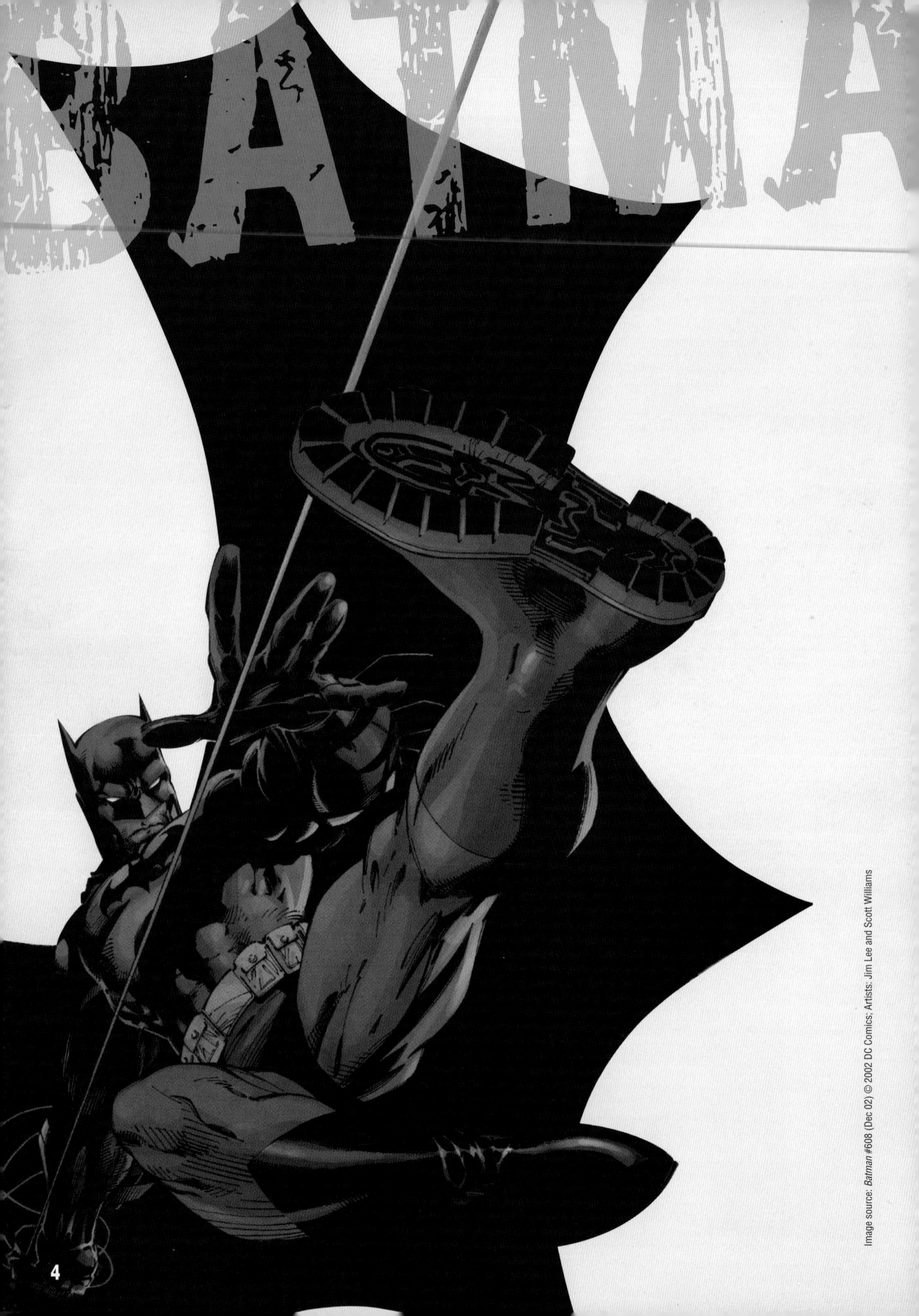
BATMA

Image source: *Batman* #608 (Dec 02) © 2002 DC Comics; Artists: Jim Lee and Scott Williams

② BATMAN

DC's ultimate tactician and planner, Batman takes a licking but keeps right on ticking. For more than 70 years, he's faced the vilest villains but continues to come out on top. Add the gritty power of a muttered "I'm Batman!" when he's in a crook's face, and he's the guy you don't want on your case.

Image source: *Batman* #627 (Jul 04) © 200≈ DC Comics; Artist: Matt Wagner

© Gutta.com

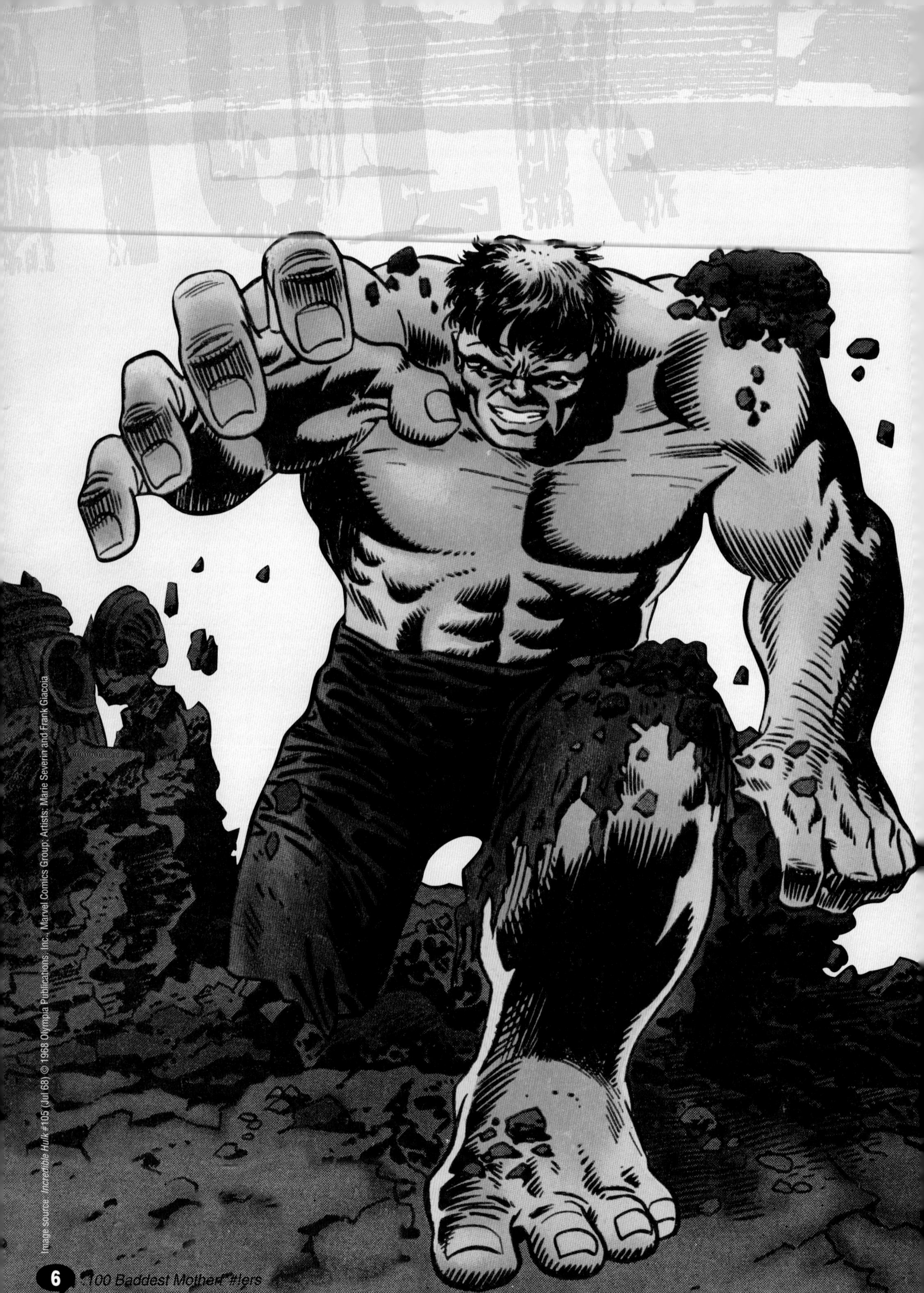

Image source: *Incredible Hulk* #105 (Jul 68) © 1968 Olympia Publications, Inc., Marvel Comics Group; Artists: Marie Severin and Frank Giacoia

❸HULK

Many only know him as a green goliath with anger management issues, but "Hulk smash!" is only *one* aspect of the multi-layered character. Over the decades, he has shown himself to be cunning, as well as savage.

❹THE JOKER

The Clown Prince of Crime's victims can only manage to smile at their fate, after The Joker unleashes his special gas. It's a weapon with which he's killed thousands in the course of his nefarious schemes. He's pointed out to The Caped Crusader that, if the Joker didn't exist, neither would Batman. He might be right.

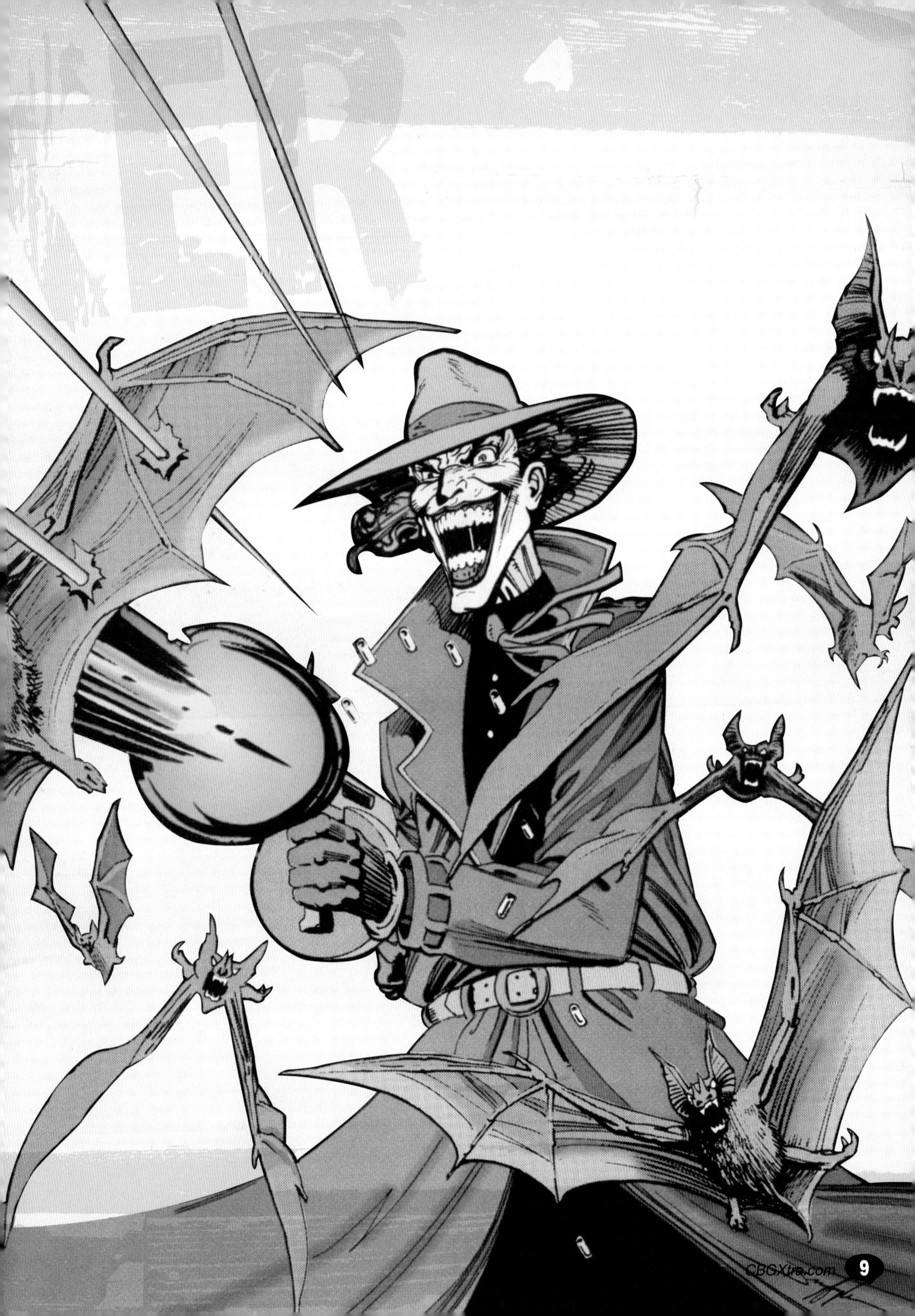

5 WOLVERINE

He's the best there is at what he does — and what he does often isn't nice. Originally, he seemed to be little more than a scrapper from Canada, but Wolverine's healing factor and "never say die" attitude have made him a fierce opponent to his enemies — and a staunch ally to his friends.

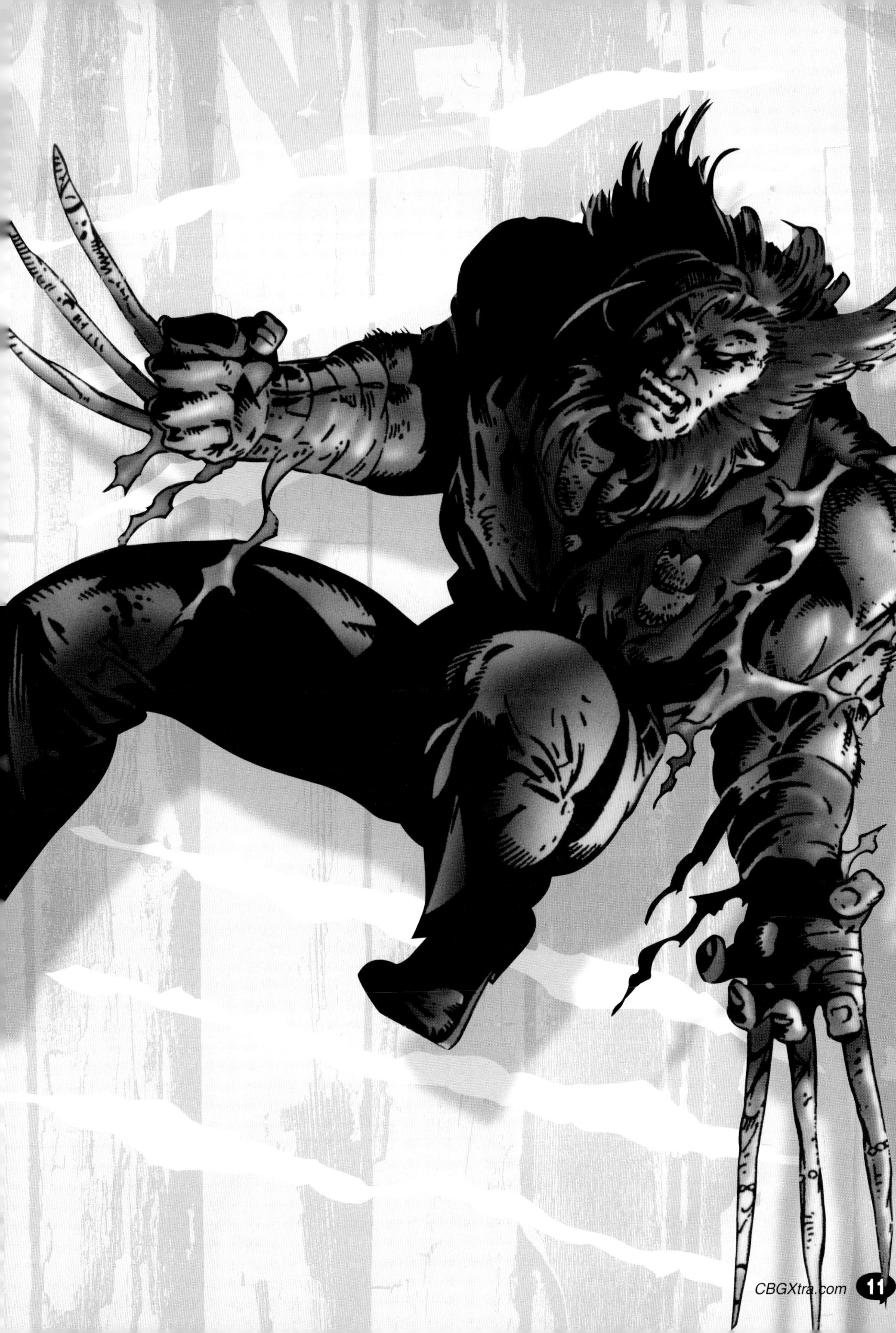

Image source: *Wolverine* #77 (Jan 94) © 1993 Marvel Entertainment Group, Inc.; Artist: Adam Kubert

Image source: Action Comics #544 (Jun 83) © 1983 DC Comics Inc.; Artist: George Pérez

₆LEX LUTHOR

With the battlesuit introduced many years ago, Luthor can sometimes stand up to Superman physcially. But it is his ability to manipulate people and events to his advantage that make the villain a formidable character. He's gone from evil scientist to ruthless businessman to U.S. President (but hasn't found a cure for baldness).

Image source: *Superman (2nd series) #49* (Nov 92) © 1992 DC Comics; Artist: Jerry Ordway

LUKE CAGE POWER MAN

With his iron-hard skin, enhanced strength, and costume straight out of '70s blaxploitation movies, Luke Cage was Marvel's hippest hero of the era. Well, if you count his catch-phrase of "Sweet Christmas" as cool. More recently, he's become a father but he's still one bad …

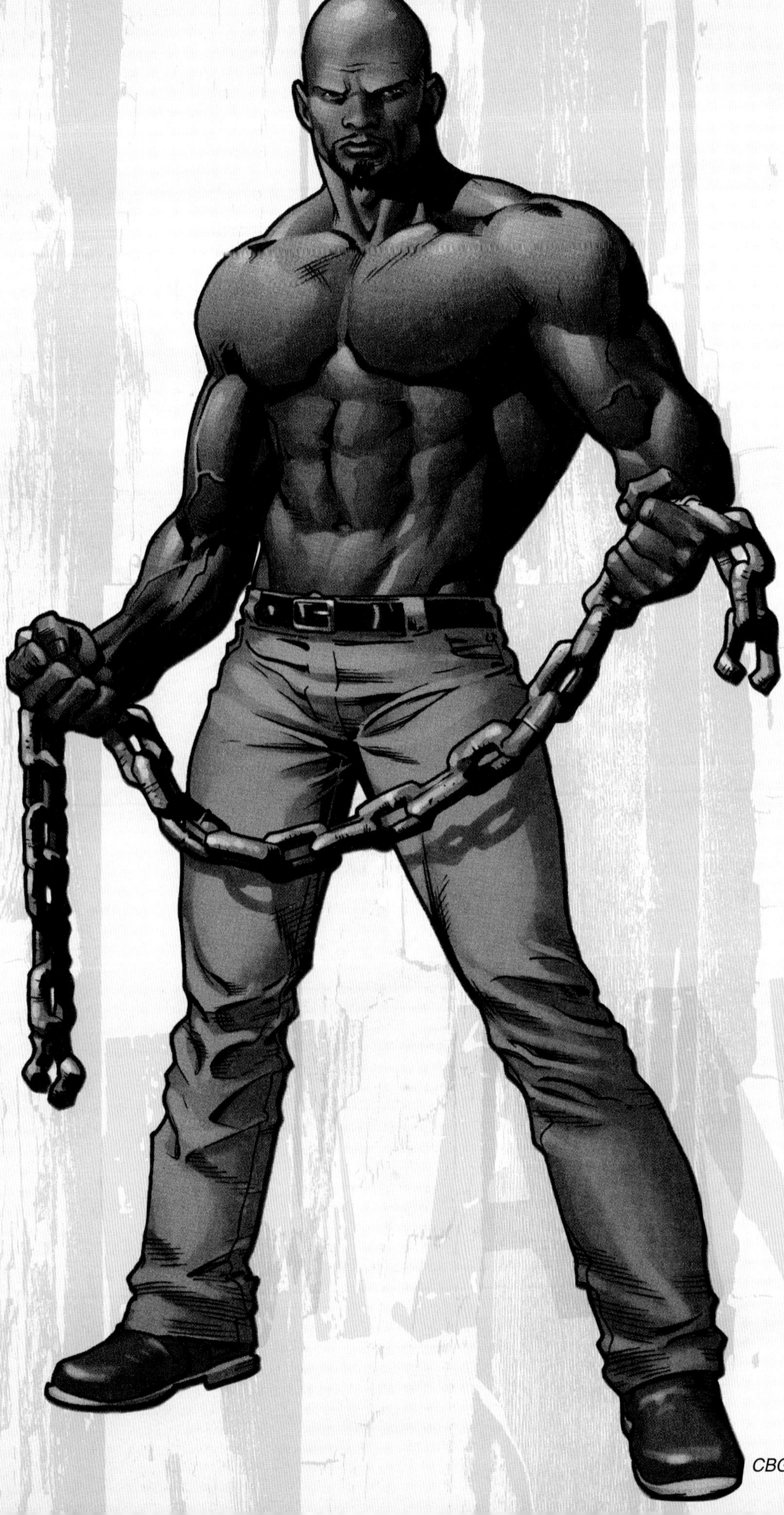

Image source: Marvel advertising for Avengers (2010) © 2010 Marvel Characters, Inc.; Artist: Unknown

8 DOCTOR DOOM

An obsession with saving his mother from the depths of Hell drove Victor von Doom to ignore Reed Richards' advice. The resultant accident not only scarred von Doom's face; it also drove him to hate his fellow genius. While he has sometimes called a truce with his longtime foes, The Fantastic Four, such truces inevitably remain in force only as long as they benefit Doctor Doom.

Image source: Fantastic Four #330 (Sep 89) © 1989 Marvel Entertainment Group, Inc.; Artists: Rich Buckler and Joe Sinnott

Baddest Mothe

9 NIGHTWING

Trained to be as tough, resourceful, and ruthless as Batman, Dick Grayson shed his Robin identity in the early 1980s to take on the darker role of Nightwing. Batman eventually sent his protégé to the crime-ridden community of Blüdhaven. There, Nightwing's career darkened to the point at which he allowed a fellow crimefighter to eliminate a foe who had plagued him. More recently, Nightwing set aside his uniform to don Batman's cape and cowl for a time.

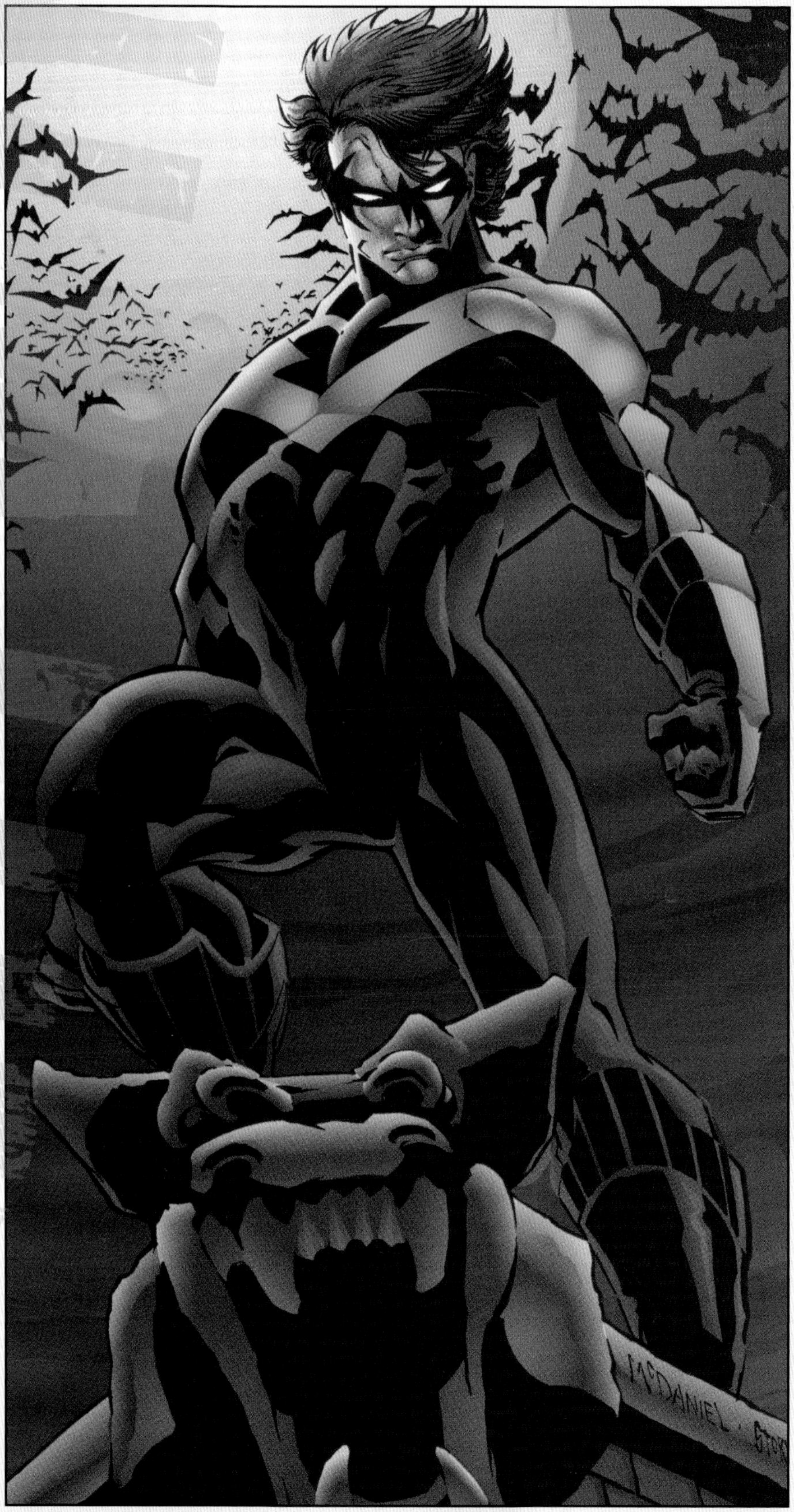
McDANIEL

Image source: *Nightwing* #2 (Nov 96) © 1996 DC Comics; Artists: Scott McDaniel and Karl Story

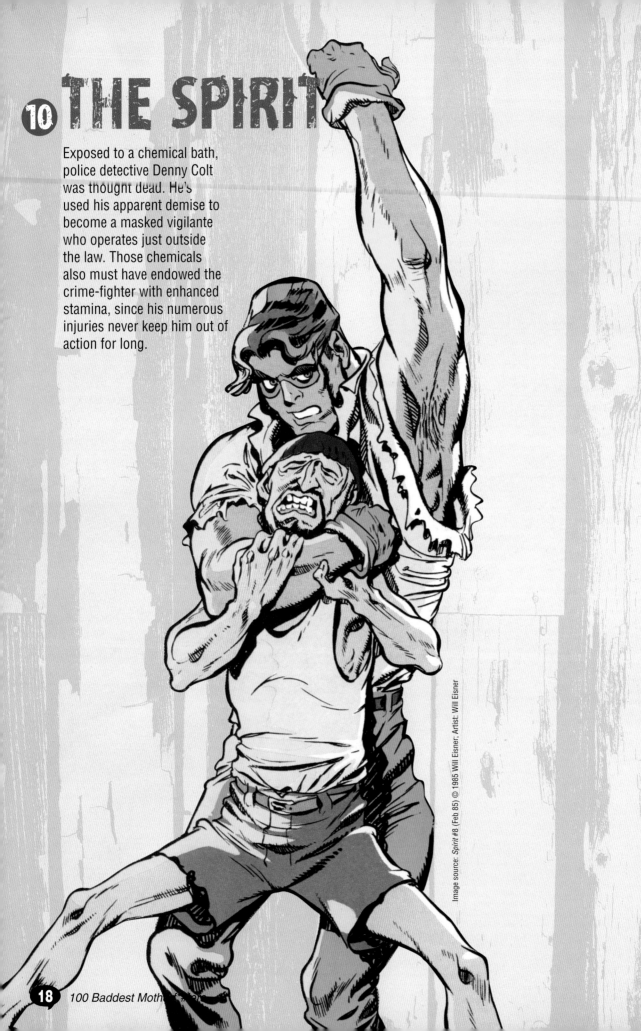

⑩ THE SPIRIT

Exposed to a chemical bath, police detective Denny Colt was thought dead. He's used his apparent demise to become a masked vigilante who operates just outside the law. Those chemicals also must have endowed the crime-fighter with enhanced stamina, since his numerous injuries never keep him out of action for long.

Image source: *Spirit* #8 (Feb 85) © 1985 Will Eisner; Artist: Will Eisner

Image source: *Daredevil* #4 (Feb 99) © 1998 Marvel Characters. Inc.; Artists: Joe Quesada and Jimmy Palmiotti

11 BULLSEYE

Able to hit any target with any projectile, the vicious Bullseye has claimed the lives of two of Daredevil's girlfriends. The cold-blooded tough guy has caused rivers of additional blood to flow on the streets of the Marvel Universe.

Image source: *Watchmen Deluxe Edition Hardcover* (1987) © 1986, 1987 DC Comics, Inc.; Artist: Dave Gibbons

12 RORSCHACH

The darkest of *Watchmen*'s many dark characters, Rorschach does whatever's necessary to take down criminal scum. The ever-changing inkblot mask that hides his identity and the muffled muttering that takes the place of articulate response provide cover for a troubled, demented crime-fighter.

⑬ COMEDIAN

Many of his missions remain classified, but what has been revealed about this character in *Watchmen* is not pretty. Adept at hand-to-hand combat as well as nearly every form of armed battle, The Comedian is a mercenary in every sense of the word.

Image source: Watchmen Deluxe Edition Hardcover (1987) © 1986, 1987 DC Comics, Inc.; Artist: Dave Gibbons

⑭ HELLBOY

As a baby demon from Hell, Hellboy was found and raised by a scientist who would go on to found the Bureau for Paranormal Research and Development. The hero wields The Right Hand of Doom as well as a number of mystically enhanced weapons in his battles with all sorts of things that go bump in the night.

Image source: Hellboy: The Crooked Man #2 (Aug 08) © 2008 Michael Mignola; Artist: Richard Corben

15 SABRETOOTH

His origins are shrouded in mystery (and will probably change many more times). Nevertheless, the fact that he's determined to make Wolverine suffer has always been clear.

Image source: *Sabretooth Classic #1* (May 94) © 1994 Marvel Entertainment Group, Inc. Artist: Dwayne Turner

Image source: *Amazing Spider-Man #60* (May 68) © 1968 Non-Pareil Publishing Corp., Marvel Comics Group; Artist: John Romita

16 KINGPIN

A master manipulator who uses his wealth and influence to gain ever more more power, The Kingpin began his career as a foe whom Spider-Man underestimated. The big man soon makes it clear that what The Web-Slinger thought at first was fat is really muscle. And, yes, he also uses his copious funds to crush his opposition. Ouch!

⑰ BLACK ADAM

An ancient Egyptian granted the powers of six of his people's gods by the wizard Shazam, Teth-Adam is the embodiment of the saying "absolute power corrupts absolutely." Maybe the old wizard should have used a more stringent vetting program for his heroes.

⑱ THE SPECTRE

Murdered police lieutenant Jim Corrigan begged for the chance to return to Earth and rescue his fianceé. His wish was granted, but with a price: He had to become the spirit of vengeance, righting injustices until he earns his heavenly reward. With his vast powers, The Spectre can move planets, stop time, and even turn bad guys into blocks of wood to be sawed up. Ewwww!

⑲ DAREDEVIL

With a father named "Battling Jack" Murdock and an attitude that earns him the nickname that becomes his super-hero nom de plume, is it any wonder that Matt Murdock won't let blindness stop him? Of course, the hyper-enhancement of his other senses, not to mention the addition of a radar sense, helps.

Image source: *Daredevil* #200 (Nov 83) © 1983 Marvel Comics Group, a division of Cadence Industries Corporation; Artists: John Byrne and Terry Austin

⑳ MAGNETO

He was the first evil mutant The X-Men faced. While he's been both an ally and an enemy in the nearly 40 years since his first appearance, Magneto's dream of mutant superiority has often blinded him to the detrimental effects of his passion.

Image source: X-Men (2nd series) #1 (Oct 91); © 1991 Marvel Entertainment Group, Inc.; Artists: Jim Lee and Scott Williams

㉑ THE CORINTHIAN

Created by The Sandman as a nightmare, that the King of Dreams destroys at the end of the story, The Corinthian is resurrected to wreak havoc on the waking world. Those eyes and his apparent lack of a soul make him super-creepy.

Image source: *The Dreaming* #18 (Nov 97) © 1997 DC Comics; Artist: Peter Doherty

㉒ KILLER CROC

A circus freak who wants to be a crimelord, Killer Croc is at least partly responsible for the creation of the second Robin, when he kills Jason Todd's parents. His continued devolution into a more reptilian state of mind makes Croc one of Batman's more dangerous foes.

Image source: *Batman* #359 (May 83) © 1983 DC Comics Inc.; Artists: Dan Jurgens and Dick Giordano

23 GHOST RIDER

A spirit of vengeance in the Marvel Universe, the aptly named Johnny Blaze makes a deal with the devil — and we all know how *those* usually turn out. The blazing skull and mystic motorcycle struck a chord with readers in the early 1970s, as horror-based comics began to return to the newsstands.

Image source: *Marvel Spotlight #6* (Oct '72) © 1972 Magazine Management Co., Inc., Marvel Comics Group — Artists: Mike Ploog and Frank Monte

24 GREEN GOBLIN

Due to a split personality, The Goblin and his alter-ego (Norman Osborn) could take *two* places on the list, but we'll settle for one. The Goblin has been the more evil of the two for the longer time. Norman has been a master manipulator, but not on the scale of Lex Luthor or The Kingpin.

Image source: *Amazing Spider-Man #39* (Aug 66) © 1966 Non-Pareil Publishing Corp.; Artists: John Romita and Mickey Demeo

₂₅ AKIRA

Image source: *Akira* Vol. 4 (2001) © 2001 Mash•Room Co. Ltd.; Artist: Katsuhiro Otomo

He doesn't look like much of a menace here, but there is a *reason* Japanese authorities keep the titular character of the long-running manga series so securely imprisoned. His mental abilities are completely off the scale: He can destroy entire cities, if he becomes sufficiently upset. You do *not* want to make him angry.

₂₆ LOBO

An intergalactic bounty hunter, Lobo takes the whole "grim and gritty" concept to the extreme. He's *so* hardcore, he's killed all the other members of his own species so that he can be "The Last Czarnian."

Image source: *Lobo Unbound* #1 (Aug 03) © 2003 DC Comics; Artist: Alex Horley

27 EVIL ERNIE

To earn the love of Lady Death, the abused Ernest Fairchild is given the mission of killing everyone on Earth. Using his supernatural powers to draw scenes that come true, Ernie takes to his quest with a vengeance. Over the course of his career, he's offed humans, demons, and even a batch of super-heroes.

28 MEPHISTO

Speaking of devils and the supernatural, how about Marvel's master schemer? Mephisto has made deals with many Marvel characters — including Spider-Man, who gives up his marriage in a compact to save Aunt May's life.

㉙ PREACHER

A bad-ass minister? Say it ain't so! Jesse Custer merges with the supernatural entity Genesis and acquires the power to command others with his voice. Teaming with former girlfriend Tulip O'Hare and Irish vampire Cassidy, Preacher faces a number of supernatural and man-made evils.

Image source: *Preacher #1* (Apr 95) © 1995 Garth Ennis and Steve Dillon; Artist: Steve Dillon

Image source: *Daredevil Comics #32* (Sep 45) © 1945 Magazine House; Artist: Charles Biro

㉚ DAREDEVIL

Unlike Marvel's Daredevil (see Page 23), *this* crimefighter is an orphan who was trained by jungle warriors and who received his costume from the tribe's chief. In his first appearance, Daredevil battled Hitler. (But why would the chief have come up with a spikey belt that means Daredevil will slash his arms every time he does calisthenics?)

31 JUDGE DREDD

He is the law in Mega City One — and has been for more than 30 years. Dredd is the ultimate judge, jury, and (when he deems appropriate) executioner. His adventures are legendary, as is his ability to overcome enemies ranging from Mean Machine Angel to Judge Death.

Image source: *Judge Dredd #1* (Nov 83) © 1983 IPC Magazines Ltd.; Artist: Brian Bolland

32 DARKNESS

Mob hitman Jackie Estacado adds to his arsenal when he turns 21 and unleashes the power of an ancient shadow soul. His new powers include creating shapes and entities as needed: an improvement from the tools he previously used to whack his enemies.

Image source: *The Darkness/Superman* #1 (Jan 05) © 2005 Top Cow Productions, Inc. and DC Comics; Artists: Tyler Kirkham and Batt

34 IRON MAN

Tony Stark initially designs his armor to escape an evil warlord. In the years since, his technical skills have made that armor a self-contained one-man army for its wearer. And Tony Stark is not the only man to don the outfit — and benefit from its advantages.

33 KID MIRACLEMAN

In the 1950s, Johnny Bates was one of Marvelman's sidekicks. He received his powers when he shouted his idol's name. When Marvelman was revived in the 1980s, the Kid turned out to be evil, and it was revealed that the earlier adventures were part of a virtual-reality program. Johnny keeps his powers when the program ends and uses them to further his own nefarious schemes. (In our real world, legal concerns from Marvel Comics caused a name change — from Marvelman to Miracleman.)

(35) DEATHSTROKE

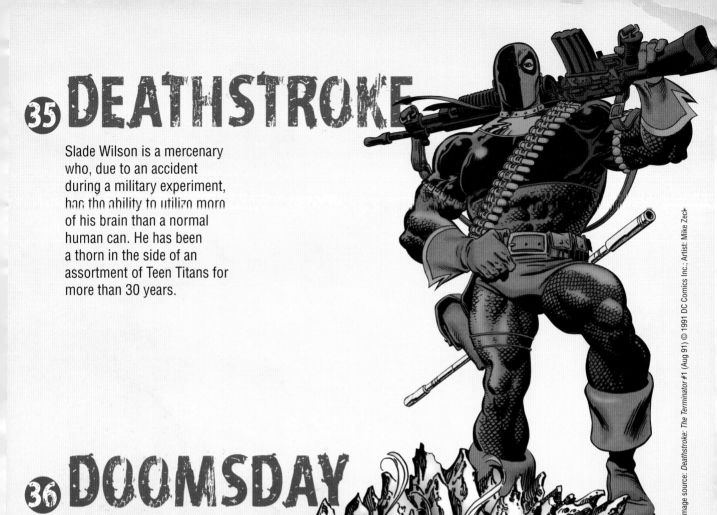

Slade Wilson is a mercenary who, due to an accident during a military experiment, has the ability to utilize more of his brain than a normal human can. He has been a thorn in the side of an assortment of Teen Titans for more than 30 years.

Image source: *Deathstroke: The Terminator* #1 (Aug 91) © 1991 DC Comics Inc.; Artist: Mike Zeck

(36) DOOMSDAY

He flattened The Justice League and severely injured several other heroes before killing Superman in 1992. But you can't keep such a force of nature down, and Doomsday has returned several times since to menace, not only The Man of Steel, but also his friends.

Image source: *Doomsday Annual* #1 (1995) © 1995 DC Ccmics; Artists: Dan Jurgens and Jerry Ordway

③⑦ ABOMINATION

Emil Blonsky exposed himself to gamma radiation in an attempt to replicate the accident that created The Hulk, but he stayed in the radiation too long and became the misshapen and aptly named Abomination. Handily beating The Hulk in their first encounter, Abomination made ol' Jade Jaws angry — and you *know* what happens when you make The Hulk angry …

Image source: *Incredible Hulk* #159 (Jan 73) © 1972 Magazine Management Co., Inc., Marvel Comics Group; Artists: Herb Trimpe and Sal Trapani

③⑧ GRENDEL

Hunter Rose is an author by day and a criminal mastermind and master assassin by night. Although several others, including Rose's granddaughter, have taken up the Grendel mantle, it's still Hunter Rose who emerges as the ultimate version of the identity.

Image source: *Grendel: Behold the Devil* #6 (Apr 08) © 2008 Matt Wagner; Artist: Matt Wagner

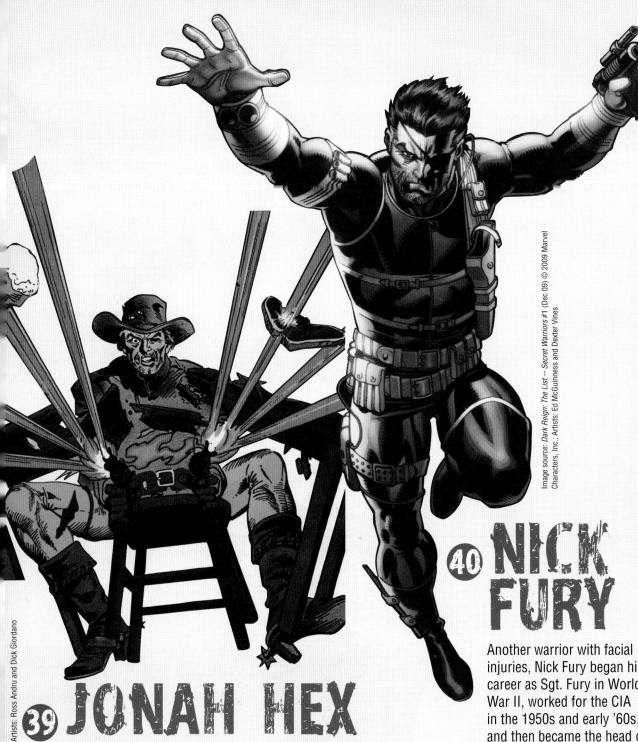

㊴ JONAH HEX

The scar-faced bounty hunter tracks down outlaws, owlhoots, and other scumbags in DC's Old West. His skills, honed in the Civil War (he still wears parts of his Confederate uniform), make him a cagy opponent. A time-trip or two to the future have shown Hex that villains are villains, no matter when they live.

㊵ NICK FURY

Another warrior with facial injuries, Nick Fury began his career as Sgt. Fury in World War II, worked for the CIA in the 1950s and early '60s, and then became the head of S.H.I.E.L.D. (The acronym has represented a variety of titles over the years.) Recently, he's assembled a secret team of ex-S.H.I.E.L.D. agents and other operatives for covert missions. His tough exterior and gruff manner are only two of the elements that make him a born leader who takes no guff from subordinates or superiors.

㊶ THE GOON

A rough-and-tumble carny, The Goon is a reluctant hero who battles supernatural menaces. You want to have him backing you up in a fight — but you do *not* want to face him, if you've ticked him off.

㊷ SOLOMON GRUNDY

Five decades after millionaire Cyrus Gold is murdered and his body dumped in Gotham City's Slaughter Swamp, his corpse is animated into the zombie-like, simple-minded Solomon Grundy. Grundy receives his name from tramps who encounter him on his first day of "life," a Monday, and recall the nursery rhyme. Composed primarily of the vegetation of his swamp origin, Grundy is a formidable foe for the Golden Age Green Lantern, whose ring can't affect wooden objects.

Image source: *The Goon* #1 (Jun 03) © 2003 Eric Powell; Artist: Eric Powell

Image source: *Infinity, Inc.* #39 (Jun 87) © 1987 DC Comics; Artists: Michael Bair, Tony DeZuniga, and Pablo Marcos

43 GREEN ARROW

Originally something of a Batman clone — with Arrow-Cave, Arrow-Car, Arrow-Plane (ouch!), and assorted arrow-based gadgets — Green Arrow turns into a fighter for social justice in the early 1970s. He's more bloodthirsty than his fellow heroes, even going so far as to kill opponents.

Image source: *Green Arrow #1* (Aug 10) © 2010 DC Comics; Artist: Mauro Cascioli

44 SINESTRO

One of the Green Lantern Corps' best and brightest, Sinestro abuses his power, using it to become a vicious overlord of his home planet. Drummed out of the Corps and banished to the anti-matter universe of Qward, Sinestro discovers the power of the yellow ring, which draws on fear. He generates plenty of that in the course of his adventures.

Image source: *Green Lantern: The Sinestro Corps War* (2007) © 2007 DC Comics; Artists: Ethan Van Sciver and Moose Baumann

㊺ IRON JAW

The Nazi criminal kills Chuck Chandler's father and kidnaps his mother. In so doing, he motivates the boy to become Crimebuster. Replacing the villain's mandible with a bear-trap prosthetic may seem like an odd choice — but it sure is creepy.

Image source: *Boy Comics #14* (Feb 44) © 1943 Magazine House, Inc; Artist: Charles Biro

㊻ SWAMP THING

Image source: *Swamp Thing #9* (Apr 74) © 1974 National Periodical Publications, Inc.; Artist: Bernie Wrightson

Originally just another muck monster, the character seems to be created when researcher Alec Holland plunges into a nearby swamp after his lab explodes, dousing him with chemicals and setting him on fire. Later, it is revealed that the character's *true* origin is that Swamp Thing is an Earth Elemental. Able to travel anywhere there is plant life and to take control of it, Swamp Thing's abilities make him a formidable foe of evil forces.

47 MARV

Sin City's prime brawler, according to his friend Dwight, Marv is "born in the wrong century. He'd be right at home on some ancient battlefield swinging an axe into somebody's face. Or in a Roman arena, taking his sword to other gladiators like him."

Image source: *Dark Horse Presents* #59 (Feb 92) © 1992 Frank Miller; Artist: Frank Miller

48 ARMSTRONG

Speaking of guys living outside their proper era: Valiant's Armstrong (shortening his original moniker of "Aram the Strong") is a near-immortal who's more interested in drinking, chasing women, and having fun than fighting. But those who cross him — or interrupt his fun — had better watch out!

ARRH! HIT ONE, IT STILL GETS ALL OVER YOU!

Image source: *Archer & Armstrong* #1 (Aug 92) © 1992 Voyager Communications Inc.; Artist: Barry Windsor-Smith

Image source: *Amazing Spider-Man #129 (Feb 74)* © 1973 Marvel Comics Group, a division of Cadence Industries Corporation; Artists: Gil Kane and John Romita

49 PUNISHER

Frank Castle is a war veteran whose family is killed when they stumble across a mob hit. In the aftermath of the tragedy, Castle assembles an armory and declares war. From time to time, his mission is sidetracked so he can help other heroes and track down other villains. Nevertheless, his bodycount should have long since wiped out any trace of the gang that started his rampage.

50 HITMAN

Contract killer Tommy Monaghan is bitten by an alien parasite; that adds x-ray vision and limited telepathy to his skills. With his new powers, Tommy turns to hunting super-heroes and supernatural threats. A side effect of his powers is a scary look caused when his corneas and irises turn as black as his pupils: It even unnerves Batman when the two first meet.

Image source: *Hitman: Ace of Killers* (2011) © 2011 DC Comics; Artist: John McCrea

51 THE THING

Marvel's original tough-guy, Ben Grimm gains a rocky exterior after a trip into space changes the friends soon to be called The Fantastic Four. His formidable form hides a heart of gold for his friends. Doesn't sound like a bad ass? Would *you* want to face a raging mad Thing bellowing, "It's clobbering time!"?

Image source: *Fantastic Four* #181 (Apr 77) © 1977 Marvel Comics Group, a division of Cadence Industries Corporation; Artists: Jack Kirby and Joe Sinnott

52 GREEN LANTERN

Hal Jordan is Earth's first member of The Green Lantern Corps and has inspired many of its members. However, when he questions the decisions of The Guardians of the Universe and turns on his fellow Corps members, turning into the time-twisting Parallax — Well, let's just say that things don't go well for his foes.

Image source: *Green Lantern* #49 (Feb 94) © 1993 DC Comics; Artists: Darryl Banks and Romeo Tanghal

53 GALACTUS

His initial appearance in *Fantastic Four* #48 (Mar 66) is supposed to be awe-inspiring, but that goofy color scheme just doesn't work for a planet-eater. No prob. The ensemble is remedied by the next issue. Wearing a purple get-up and more of a force of nature than an actual *villain*, Galactus' constant cosmic hunger makes him an intergalactic threat.

Image source: *Fantastic Four* #48 (Mar 66) © 1966 Canam Publisher Sales Corp.; Artists: Jack Kirby and Joe Sinnott

54 THE HEAP

When the biplane of World War I German flying ace Baron Eric von Emmelman crashes into a swamp, he clings to a spark of life while his body decays and merged with the vegetation. In World War II, he returns as The Heap, where he turns on his countrymen and their Nazi affiliations, eventually wandering the globe battling supernatural menaces. What *is* it with mindless swamp monsters and their need to wander?

Image source: *Airboy Comics* #85 (Vol. 9 #12, Jan 53) © 1952 Hillman Periodicals, Inc.; Artist: Ernest Schroeder

55 THE MAXX

In the imaginary world of The Outback, The Maxx protects The Jungle Queen. In the real world, he's a homeless outcast, and The Jungle Queen is a social worker who bails him out of trouble. The duo's run-ins in *both* worlds with such characters as serial killer Mr. Gone give the series its edge.

56 THANOS

The son of Eternals Mentor and Sui-San, Thanos is obsessed with death since his early days, an obsession which leads to his wooing of Mistress Death. As part of his attempted romance, he acquires The Infinity Gauntlet and destroys half of all life in the Marvel Universe. (His weakness lies in the fact that such power is beyond his capabilities to handle.)

57 DOCTOR OCTOPUS

One of Spider-Man's earliest foes, atomic researcher Otto Octavius bonded remote-control arms to himself in an accident. A brilliant scientist, Ock has been behind some of Spider-Man's most memorable stories, up to and including an almost-wedding to Aunt May. Can you say, "Uncle Otto"?

Image source: *Amazing Spider-Man* #89 (Oct 70) © 1970 Magazine Management Co., Inc., Marvel Comics Group; Artists: Gil Kane and John Romita

58 DEADPOOL

Don't underestimate disfigured mercenary Wade Wilson. Despite his humorous asides and breaking the fourth wall to talk directly to readers, Deadpool combines superior athletic and combat skills with a healing factor. He is a force to be reckoned with.

Image source: *Deadpool* #4 (Jan 09) © 2008 Marvel Characters, Inc.; Artist: Jason Pearson

59 REVERSE-FLASH

The 25th century's Lobard Thawne has been responsible for at least two tragedies in The Flash's life: Thawne murdered both Barry Allen's wife and mother. Reverse-Flash has mastered both speed and time-travel, making him a villain who can appear anywhere at any time.

"I RAN *HARD*, GENERATING ENOUGH NEGATIVE ENERGY--

60 SUB-MARINER

Prince Namor is one of Marvel's earliest heroes, appearing in *Marvel Comics* #1 in 1939. Blaming surface people for damage to his undersea kingdom, he attacked New York at first, then took on the Nazis during World War II. In the years since, his resentment of the surface world has deepened, bringing him into conflict with The Fantastic Four numerous times. His volatile nature means another attack could occur at any time.

61 KICK-ASS

Dave Lizewski dons a modified wetsuit, covers his head, and goes on patrol to fight crimo. Though a trio of robbers gives him an ass-kicking, rather than vice versa, he recovers. Honing his skills, Dave becomes a successful hero, finding that other vigilantes can show him how ruthless he has to be to survive.

Image source: *Kick-Ass* #8 (Mar 10) © 2010 Mark Millar and John S. Romita; Artists: John Romita Jr. and Tom Palmer

62 ORION

Darkseid's son is sent to New Genesis in an exchange between that world and Apokolips. Raised to follow the ways of peace, Orion manages his anger and becomes a powerful warrior, able to stand up to such heroes as Superman. His dark nature, however, eventually pulls him back to Apokolips, where he faces his father.

Image source: *New Gods* #1 (Mar 71) © 1971 National Periodical Publications, Inc.; Artists: Jack Kirby and Vince Colletta

63 MAN-THING

Swamp-dweller Man-Thing has an origin typical for swamp-dwelling fantasy monsters. Researcher Ted Hallis attempts to re-create the Super-Soldier Formula that gave Captain America his abilities, when a lab accident occurs near a swamp. Diving into the water, Hallis comes out a muck monster. However, this pile of shambling ick has an added twist: Those who fear him burn when Man-Thing touches them. It'd be pretty hard *not* to be scared with this guy coming after you, right? (Let's not even get started on his name, especially when Marvel adds the word *Giant-Size* to his adventures' title.)

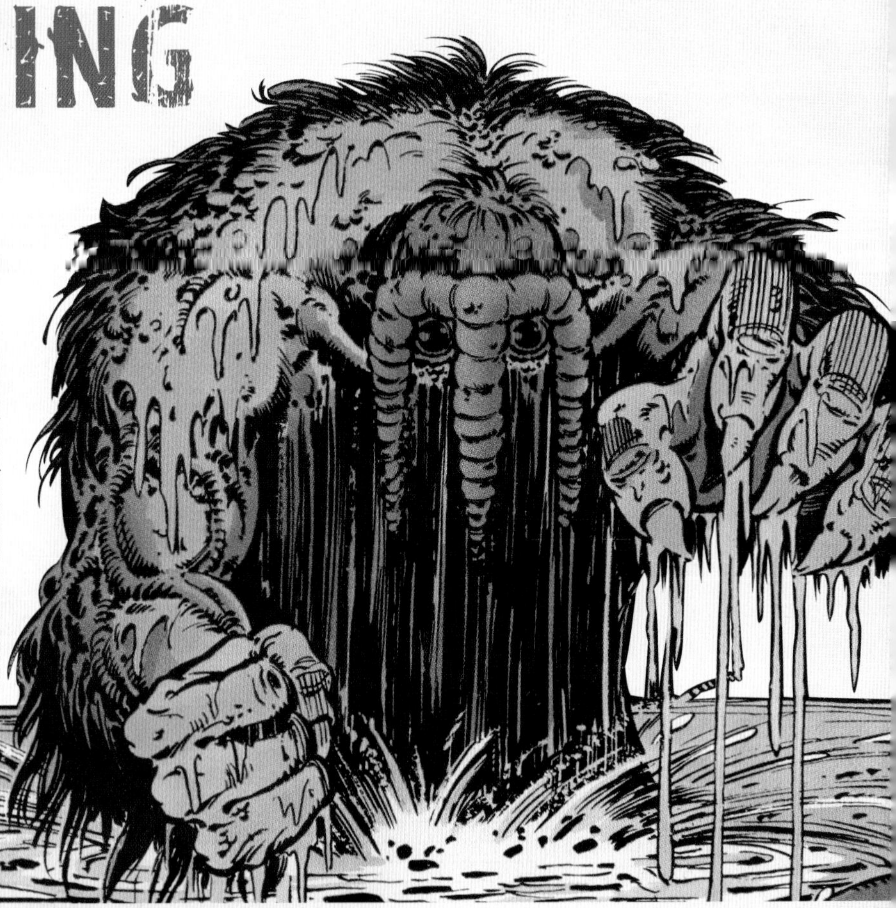

Image source: *Man-Thing* #1 (Nov 79) © 1979 Marvel Comics Gro division of Cadence Industries Corporation; Artist: Bob Wiacek

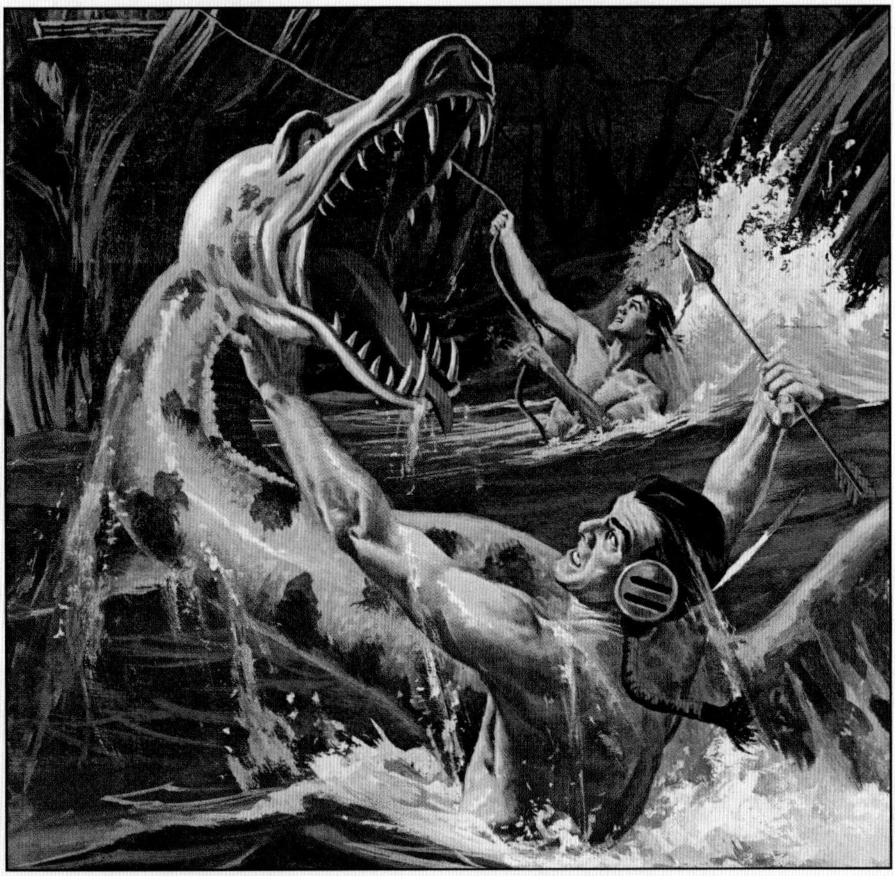

Image source: *Turok, Son of Stone* #47 (Sep 65) © 1965 Western Publishing Company, Inc.; Artists: Uncredited

64 TUROK

Take on a dinosaur with a bow and arrow or a flint knife? That's hardcore, but Native American Turok and his young companion, Andar, do so after they discover a lost land where dinosaurs still live alongside other dangers. The two warriors find a poison that makes their arrows effective against the largest menaces, as they strive to survive while hunting for a way home.

65 JOHNNY THE HOMICIDAL MANIAC

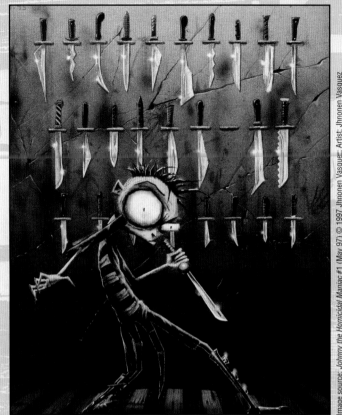

His name should suffice to describe the character, but keep in mind that Johnny's homicidal rages can be triggered by almost anything that bugs him. That includes such words as "wacky." Fortunately, that word is unlikely to occur to those trying to describe him accurately. Brrr.

Image source: *Johnny the Homicidal Maniac #1* (May 97) © 1997 Jhnonen Vasquez; Artist: Jhnonen Vasquez

66 PROMETHEUS

A twisted villain with numerous origin stories (most of which he makes up himself), Prometheus' implant allows him to download information on his foes. Yes, that includes the best ways to defeat those enemies. He has successfully taken on the entire Justice League single-handedly several times.

Image source: *JLA #17* (Apr 98) © 1998 DC Comics; Artists: Arnie Jorgensen, David Meikis, and Mark Pennington

⁶⁷ LOKI

Thor's half-brother has come up with a number of nefarious schemes, and he loves to make his Asgardian sibling look bad. Loki's command of dark magic, coupled with a lust for ultimate power on the throne of Asgard, make him a power player.

Image source: *Thor* #175 (Apr 70) © 1970 Magazine Management Co., Inc.; Marvel Comics Group; Artists: Marie Severin and John Verpoorten

⁶⁸ BLACK HOOD

Several characters have donned the cursed executioner's headgear and become The Black Hood. Unfortunately, the curse cuts each career short, since they are doomed to die after a short time. Maybe it's time to think more carefully before making a career choice. Just a suggestion …

Image source: *Black Hood* #7 (Jul 92) © 1992 Archie Comic Publications, Inc.; Artist: Rick Burchett

69 RICK GRIMES

The Walking Dead's focal character, Sheriff Grimes is shot in the line of duty and lapses into a coma. When he wakes, he finds the hospital deserted and his family gone. Shortly after he starts searching for them, he encounters the first in a long line of zombies. Ever since, he's shown no mercy to the dead — or the living who cross him. Even losing a hand hasn't slowed him down.

70 BLACK PANTHER

Wakandan war chief T'Challa is the latest in a line of a Black Panthers whose legacy stretches back centuries. Embued with the panther spirit and his country's superior technology, T'Challa has taken the defense of his country global.

(71) BISHOP

A mutant bounty hunter from a future in which mutants are hunted, Bishop comes to the 20th century and reluctantly joins The X-Men. After years of trying to fit in, he finally reveals his true colors, becoming the mutants' enemy and a fierce foe.

Image source: *Uncanny X-Men* #288 (May 92) © 1992 Marvel Entertainment Group, Inc.; Artist: Andy Kubert

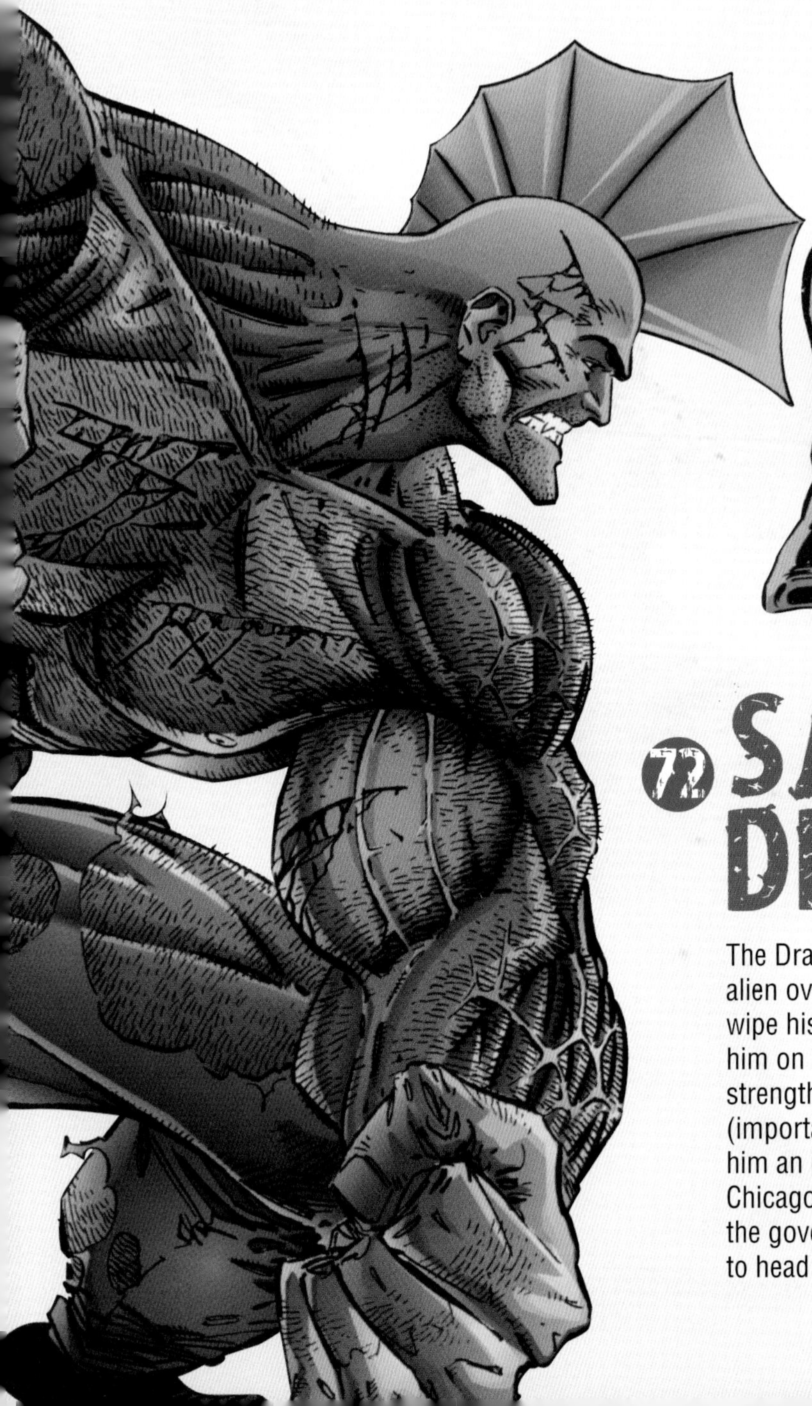

(72) SAVAGE DRAGON

The Dragon is a deposed alien overlord whose subjects wipe his memory and strand him on Earth. His superior strength and healing abilities (important in a brawler) make him an important member of Chicago's police force before the government recruits him to head a team of heroes.

Image source: *Savage Dragon* #16 (Jan 95) © 1995 Erik Larsen; Artist: Erik Larsen

73 SPAWN

Deceased mercenary Alex Simmons works a deal with the devil in order to return to Earth and the love of his life, Wanda. But there's a price to pay. The devil makes him the latest in a series of Hellspawn: disfigured, demonic officers in Hell's army. After a number of heroic actions, Spawn is badly hurt and further mutilated by The Redeemer, yet he continues his fight.

Image source: *Spawn* #24 (Sep 94) © 1994 Todd McFarlane Productions, Inc. Artist: Todd McFarlane

74 BLADE

When his mother is attacked by vampire Deacon Frost while he is being born, Eric Brooks acquires vampiric abilities, long life, and a sense for supernatural creatures. He uses these powers with his fighting skills, acquired over more than a century, to hunt down such creatures of the night as Dracula.

Image source: *Blade* #2 (Dec 06) © 2006 Marvel Characters, Inc.; Artist: Marko Djurdjevic

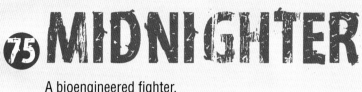

⑦⑤ MIDNIGHTER

A bioengineered fighter, Midnighter can sense an opponent's moves before that foe can make them. He also has healing abilities. (Does *every* brawler have those? But that's a topic for another day.) His marriage to the super-powered Apollo hasn't mellowed him. If anything, calling attention to his preferences is asking for trouble.

Image source: *Midnighter* # 6 (Apr 03) © 2008 WildStorm Productions, an imprint of DC Comics; Artists: Lee Garbett and Trevor Scott

Image source: *Official Handbook of the Marvel Universe Master Edition Vol. 5* (1987) © 1987 Marvel Entertainment Group, Inc.; Artist: Bill Sienkiewicz

⑦⑥ MOON KNIGHT

Marc Spector is a former mercenary who uses his fortune to fight crime. In that role, he's developed other identities; that's given him multiple personalities. A bite from a werewolf gives him additional strength, based on the cycles of the moon. Bad guys should hope for a lunar eclipse.

Image source: *Badger* #1 (1983) © 1983 Capital Publications, Inc.; Artists: Steve Rude and Jeffrey Butler

(77) BADGER

Norbert Sykes is a Vietnam veteran suffering from multiple personality disorder. Institutionalized near Madison, Wis., Norbert escapes and meets a fifth-century druid who unleashes the full potential of Norbert's Badger personality. The urban vigilante is as dangerous as his namesake (who's also the mascot for the University of Wisconsin-Madison, as well as the official state animal).

Image source: *Thor* #229 (Nov 74) © 1974 Marvel Comics Group, a division of Cadence Industries Corporation; Artists: Ron Wilson and Mike Esposito

(78) THOR

A rebellious troublemaker in his early days, Thor is cast out of Asgard in an effort by his father, Odin, to teach him humility. After regaining his powers, Thor battles the forces of evil, enjoying a good fight alongside his friends against Asgard's enemies. His strength, courage, and powerful hammer have made him a match for such cosmic entities as Galactus.

⑦⑨ MAJOR FORCE

Clifford Zmeck is offered a pardon for his life sentence, if he participates in an experiment with an alien metal. With more of the other-worldly substance used than that which created Captain Atom, Major Force is bigger and stronger than the Captain and wields a dark energy different from Atom's energy bolts. While the Army initially tries to style him as a hero, Major Force's true nature quickly comes to the fore. Among his victims is Green Lantern Kyle Rayner's girlfriend.

FREE! I'M FINALLY FREE!!!

Image source: *Captain Atom* #35 (Nov 89) © 1989 DC Comics, Inc.; Artists: Rafael Kayanan and Romeo Tanghal

Image source: *Captain America* #103 (Jul 68) © 1968 Leading Magazine Corp., Marvel Comics Group; Artists: Jack Kirby and Syd Shores

⑧⓪ RED SKULL

Handpicked by Hitler to be a symbol of the Nazi regime, The Red Skull is the top evil agent of World War II, clashing again and again with Captain America. Trapped in a bunker in the last days of the war, The Skull revives years later to continue his schemes for world domination: schemes far more grand than those of Hitler.

81 GOLGO 13

The Japanese hitman, also known as Duke Togo, is on the most-wanted lists of several intelligence organizations around the world. He uses a modified M-16 for many of his missions but is an expert in a variety of firearms and other weapons.

Image source: *Golgo 13 Vol. 1: Supergun* (2006) © 2006 Saito Production and Viz Media, LLC; Artist: Takao Saito

82 IBAC

Lucifer gives small-time crook Stanley "Stinky" Printwhistle the powers of four of history's worst villains (**I**van the Terrible, Cesare **B**orgia, **A**ttila the Hun, and **C**aligula) in an attempt to defeat Captain Marvel. Unable to do so in his first outing, Printwhistle reforms but is repeatedly tricked or coerced into saying the magic word "IBAC." Doing so gives him super-human strength and stamina nearly equal to Cap's.

Image source: *Justice League of America* #135 (Oct 76) © 1976 National Periodical Publications, Inc.; Artists: Dick Dillin and Frank McLaughlin

NOW, *SPY SMASHER*... IT'S *MY* TURN TO HIT *YOU!*

BUT--UNLIKE ME-- *SPY SMASHER* WILL FEEL *THIS* PUNCH-- I *GUARANTEE* IT!

(83) TASKMASTER

His ability to mimic the fighting style of any hero or villain once he's seen it makes him a formidable opponent on his own. However, Taskmaster has made more of his reputation by hiring out as a trainer to others.

Image source: *Avengers: The Initiative* #33 (Apr 10) © 2010 Marvel Characters, Inc.; Artist: David Yardin

(84) OCTOPUS

Like Moriarty in the world of Sherlock Holmes, The Octopus is something of a "Napoleon of Crime." One of the few characters in comics who has never been fully shown, he battles The Spirit almost to a standstill several times throughout his career. Please wipe images of The Octopus from *The Spirit* movie (2009) from your mind.

Image source: *Spirit* section (Aug. 10, 1947) © 1947 Everett M. Arnold; Artist: Will Eisner

85 OZYMANDIAS

His abilities include sharpened brain power and reflexes, and his skills make him a hero to some. On the other hand, his Machiavellian schemes turn his fellow heroes against him in *Watchmen*.

Image source: *Watchmen* #6 (Aug 86) © 1986 DC Comics, Inc.; Artist: Dave Gibbons

86 DOCTOR LIGHT

For years, Doctor Light seems little more than a minor villain who employs an assortment of light-based gimmicks. But his true, vile nature is revealed in *Identity Crisis*, as well as the reason he has been such a loser. (On the other hand, you have to give the guy's earlier appearances *some* props for taking on members of The Justice League by himself.)

Image source: *The Atom* #8 (Sep 63) © 1963 National Periodical Publications, Inc.; Artists: Gil Kane and Murphy Anderson

87 VENOM

Forced off Spider-Man, the alien symbiote that has been his costume bonds with disgraced photographer Eddie Brock. Together, the two stalk The Web-Slinger. With with the ability to avoid detection by his arch-enemy and posessed of powers mimicking those of Spidey, Venom threatens his foe's very existence.

Image source: *Venom: Lethal Protector* #5 (Jun 93) © 1993 Marvel Entertainment Group, Inc.; Artists: Mark Bagley and Sam de la Rosa

88 SUPREME

Depending on which history you follow, Supreme is either the product of a scientific experiment, a teen who's had a run-in with a meteor composed of Supremium, or a fallen god. Whichever origin is the case, Supreme is not afraid to get his hands bloody in his battles with evil denizens of the Image Universe.

Image source: *Supreme* #41 (Aug 96) © 1996 Rob Liefeld, Inc.; Artists: Joe Bennett and Marlo Alquiza

Image source: *Violator* #1 (May 94) © 1994 Todd McFarlane Productions, Inc. Artist: Bradley Oer

89 VIOLATER

The oldest of five demons whose mission is to guide Hellspawns in their training for Hell's army, Violator appears as a clown in *Spawn*. But there's nothing funny about him, especially when he assumes a more demonic aspect.

90 CABLE

Cyclops and Jean Grey's son, Nathan, returns from the future where he's been raised, sporting a bionic arm and eye as well as advanced weaponry. His less-tolerant nature in leading The New Mutants quickly turns that team of young heroes-in-training into the first incarnation of X-Force. He's willing to do what needs to be done to save mutant-kind, no matter how distasteful he finds it.

Image source: *Cable* #5 (Sep 08) © 2008 Marvel Characters, Inc.; Artist: Ariel Olivetti

91 SIVANA

The world's maddest scientist, Thaddous Bodog Sivana's ultimate dream of world domination, aided by his various evil discoveries, is in constant conflict with Fawcett's Captain Marvel (or, as Sivana calls him, "The Big Red Cheese").

Image source: *Captain Marvel Adventures* #100 (Sep 49) © 1949 Fawcett Publications, Inc.; Artist: C.C. Beck

Image source: *The Avengers: Kang -- Time and Time Again* (2005) © 2005 Marvel Characters, Inc.; Artist: John Buscema

92 KANG THE CONQUEROR

The twists and turns of the time-traveling Kang's origins can make one's head hurt, but he has been a menace for The Avengers for years. (In the midst of the headache, of course, the reader wonders why, after a given defeat, Kang doesn't return to the future, recover, and return to a moment just after that defeat, when he could win the day. He may be long on scheming but short on smarts.)

93 HELLBLAZER

A born con-man, John Constantine is a reluctant hero in the magical community. Confronting countless fantastic threats, he has manipulated his way out of them — going so far as to to cure his cancer by making a deal with the devil.

Image source: *Hellblazer* #83 (Nov 94) © 1994 DC Comics; Artist: Glenn Fabry

Image source: *Official Handbook of the Marvel Universe A-Z Vol. 5* (2008) © 2008 Marvel Characters, Inc.; Artist: Mark Pacella

94 JACKAL

Professor Miles Warren lets his lust for Gwen Stacy spiral out of control until he gains a split personality. His evil side takes on the moniker of The Jackal. While his costume doesn't look much like that of his namesake, his cunning (which lets him go so far as to make Spider-Man clones) mirrors that of the animal.

Image source: *Incredible Hulk* #342 (Apr 88) © 1988 Marvel Entertainment Group, Inc.; Artist: Todd McFarlane

95 THE LEADER

Accidentally exposed to gamma radiation, Samuel Sterns finds that his mental (not his physical) prowess has increased exponentially. Discarding his name, Sterns takes on the title he aims to achieve. Unfortunately for him, it seems that, in going up against The Hulk, brawn beats brains every time. Eventually, he destroys a town of 5,000 with a gamma bomb and recruits the irradiated survivors to his army.

96 ECLIPSO

Originally the dark side of solar researcher Bruce Gordon, Eclipso is reborn as an evil schemer who was the Spirit of Vengeance before The Spectre but was removed from that post when he became *too* vengeful. His actions lead to deaths of some of his enemies, though his attempts to turn heroes evil come to naught.

Image source: *House of Secrets* #72 (Jun 65) © 1965 National Periodical Publications, Inc.; Artist: Jack Sparling

97 HATE MONGER

Nick Fury tricks The Fantastic
Four into going to South
America to defeat this villain,
who manipulates emotions
of those around him with
his ray gun. Revealed as
Hitler (or a lookalike), Hate
Monger comes into conflict
with Fury several more times,
increasing the power and
range of his hate ray, until it
becomes an orbiting satellite.

Image source: *Marvel Collector's Item Classics* #15 (Jun 68) © 1968 Animated Timely
Features, Inc., Marvel Comics Group; Artists: Jack Kirby and George Roussos

98 THE CLAW

A mysterious being who
commands an army of pirates
in the Pacific during World
War II, The Claw is known
there as "The God of Hate."
His bony, taloned hands,
sharp teeth, evil face, and
ability to grow as tall as a
skyscraper make him an
imposing foe for both Silver
Streak and Lev Gleason's
original Daredevil.

Image source: *Daredevil Comics* #15 (Feb 42) © 1942 Comic House, Inc.; Artist: Bob Wood

99 CARRION

No relation to the later Spider-Man villain, Carrion is a schemer and con man who frequently runs afoul of The Spirit. His ability to escape justice, often aided by his pet vulture Julia, makes him a memorable foe who refuses to quit.

Image source: *Spirit #6* (Aug 84) © 1984 Will Eisner; Artist: Will Eisner

100 M.O.D.O.K.

A big floating head in a mobility chair may not seem like much of a menace, but the Mental Organism Designed Only for Killing (yeah, M.O.D.O.F.K. doesn't have the same zing), is no mental midget. His brain blasts even bring The Hulk to his knees. However, knock M.O.D.O.K. on his back, and he's going to have a hard time getting up without help.

Image source: *Super-Villain Team-Up: Modok's 11 #1* (Sep 07) © 2007 Marvel Characters, Inc.; Artist: Eric Powell

THEY MADE THE MOTHERF*#!ERS!

Many fine artists from the 1930s to today have provided striking images of rough, tough characters — some of which they originated, some of which they re-imagined. These creators produced the images in this book, and we thank them all for their memorable work.

Mario Alquiza	Supremo
Murphy Anderson	Doctor Light
Ross Andru	Jonah Hex
Jim Aparo	Spectre
Terry Austin	Daredevil, Joker
Mark Bagley	Venom
Michael Bair	Solomon Grundy
Darryl Banks	Green Lantern
Carl Barks	Uncle Scrooge
Eddy Barrows	Black Adam
Batt	Darkness
Moose Baumann	Sinestro
C.C. Beck	Sivana
Joe Bennett	Supreme
Charles Biro	Daredevil, Iron Jaw
Brian Bolland	Judge Dredd
Norm Breyfogle	Joker
Rich Buckler	Doctor Doom, Sub-Mariner
Rick Burchett	Black Hood
John Buscema	Kang
Jeffrey Butler	Badger
John Byrne	Daredevil
Mauro Cascioli	Green Arrow
Dave Cockrum	Hulk, Luke Cage (Power Man)
Vince Colletta	Orion
Richard Corben	Hellboy
Sam de la Rosa	Venom
Tony DeZuniga	Solomon Grundy
Dick Dillin	Ibac
Steve Dillon	Jesse Custer (Preacher)
Marko Djurdjevic	Blade, Mephisto
Peter Doherty	Corinthian
Will Eisner	Carrion, Octopus, Spirit
Mike Esposito	Thor, Green Goblin
Glenn Fabry	Hellblazer
Lee Garbett	Midnighter
Frank Giacoia	Hulk
Dave Gibbons	Comedian, Ozymandias, Rorschach
Keith Giffen	Black Adam
Dick Giordano	Jonah Hex, Killer Croc
Dan Green	Black Adam
Alex Horley	Lobo
Arnie Jorgensen	Prometheus
Dan Jurgens	Doomsday, Killer Croc
Gil Kane	Doctor Light, Doctor Octopus, Punisher
Rafael Kayanan	Major Force
Sam Kieth	Maxx
Jack Kirby	Darkseid, Galactus, Hate Monger, Orion, Red Skull, Thing
Tyler Kirkham	Darkness
Andy Kubert	Bishop
Adam Kubert	Wolverine
Erik Larsen	Savage Dragon
Bob Layton	Iron Man
Jim Lee	Batman, Magneto
Eric Mache	Evil Ernie
Pablo Marcos	Solomon Grundy
John McCrea	Hitman
Scott McDaniel	Nightwing
Todd McFarlane	Leader, Spawn
Ed McGuinness	Nick Fury
Frank McLaughlin	Ibac
Bob McLeod	Sub-Mariner
David Meikis	Prometheus
Frank Miller	Marv, Wolverine
Frank Monte	Ghost Rider
Tony Moore	Rick Grimes
Bradley Ober	Violator
Ariel Olivetti	Cable
Jerry Ordway	Doomsday, Lex Luthor
Katsuhiro Otomo	Akira
Mark Pacella	Jackal
Tom Palmer	Kick-Ass
Jimmy Palmiotti	Bullseye
Jason Pearson	Deadpool
Mark Pennington	Prometheus
George Pérez	Darkseid, Lex Luthor, Thanos
Mike Ploog	Ghost Rider
Eric Powell	Goon, M.O.D.O.K.
Joe Quesada	Bullseye
Rodney Ramos	Black Adam
John Ridgway	Kid Miracleman
Marshall Rogers	Joker
John Romita	Doctor Octopus, Green Goblin, Kingpin, Luke Cage (Power Man), Punisher
John Romita Jr.	Iron Man, Kick-Ass
George Roussos	Hate Monger
Steve Rude	Badger
Takao Saito	Golgo 13
Ernest Schroeder	Heap
Trevor Scott	Midnighter
Marie Severin	Hulk, Loki
Tony Shasteen	Darkseid
Syd Shores	Red Skull
Bill Sienkiewicz	Moon Knight
Joe Sinnott	Doctor Doom, Galactus, Thing
Jack Sparling	Eclipso
Karl Story	Nightwing
Romeo Tanghal	Green Lantern, Major Force
Bruce Timm	Black Panther
Sal Trapani	Abomination
Herb Trimpe	Abomination
Dwayne Turner	Sabretooth
Ethan van Sciver	Reverse Flash, Sinestro
Jhonen Vasquez	Johnny the Homicidal Maniac
Rick Veitch	Kid Miracleman
John Verpoorten	Loki
Dexter Vines	Nick Fury
Matt Wagner	Batman, Grendel
Bob Wiacek	Man-Thing
Scott Williams	Batman, Magneto
Ron Wilson	Thor
Barry Windsor-Smith	Armstrong
Bob Wood	Claw
Bernie Wrightson	Swamp Thing
David Yardin	Taskmaster
Mike Zeck	Deathstroke